Foreword to the first printing
August 1986

This pamphlet tells part of the story of the Hormel company's insatiable lust for "profits at all costs" and how a group of people decide that concessions are not the answer and that they will fight back against all odds.

Despite these odds—the company town, the company-controlled local police, the Minnesota National Guard, the biased court system, and the betrayal by the United Food and Commercial Workers International Union—the fighting P-9ers and their supporters are continuing their struggle until all are back to work.

The unprecedented aid and solidarity of many religious, civic, and labor organizations has made the boycott of Hormel products felt throughout the world.

This pamphlet deserves your consideration, because our struggle is one that every working person who has felt the sting of concessions can identify with. And to those who have not yet felt this degradation of their dignity, we are people who have decided that enough is enough.

Jim Guyette,
President, United Food
and Commercial Workers
Local P-9

Author's note

The material in this pamphlet is based on research and observations in Austin, Minnesota, in the spring and summer of 1986. In developing this story I have relied heavily on personal interviews with members of United Food and Commercial Workers Local P-9, who were generous with their time.

For historical background I have also used written materials, including two books: *In Quest of Quality—Hormel's First 75 Years* by Richard Dougherty (Austin, Mn.: Geo. A. Hormel & Co., 1966) and *Toward a Democratic Work Process; The Hormel Packinghouse Workers' Experiment* by Fred H. Blum (New York: Harper, 1953).

Particularly helpful was an as-yet unpublished paper delivered at the 1986 Missouri Valley History Conference

Jim Guyette with Karen Lantz, leader of striking TWA flight attendants, at New York solidarity rally of 1,000 on March 14, 1986.

March 15 in Omaha, Nebraska, entitled, *The Austin Orbit: Regional Union Organizing in Meat Packing, 1933–1943,* by Rick Halpern, Department of History, University of Pennsylvania, and Roger Horowitz, Department of History, University of Wisconsin-Madison.

I have also relied on current union documents. Where these are quoted directly, the source is given. I have frequently cited a May 16, 1986, affidavit submitted to a federal court by Local P-9 President Jim Guyette. This document was part of an appeal asking the U.S. District Court for Minnesota to block implementation of the UFCW International officials' trusteeship over the local earlier that month. Guyette's affidavit gives a detailed account of the struggle by Local P-9 and other locals against attacks by Hormel, and of the efforts of top UFCW officials to sabotage that fight.

Where participants such as Jim Guyette are quoted without a source being cited, it is from a personal interview.

A chronology of major events mentioned in these pages appears at the end of the pamphlet.

The rendering of all this material is my own responsibility, as are any errors.

Fred Halstead
July 29, 1986

Striking Hormel workers confront scabs in winter 1986.

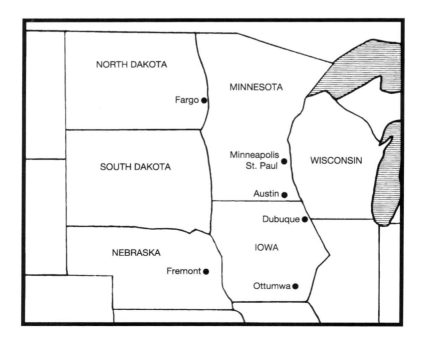

NORTH DAKOTA

MINNESOTA

Fargo ●

SOUTH DAKOTA

Minneapolis
St. Paul ●

WISCONSIN

Austin ●

Dubuque ●

NEBRASKA

IOWA

Fremont ●

Ottumwa ●

The 1985–86
Hormel meat-packers strike
in Austin, Minnesota

On August 17, 1985, the 1,500 union meat-packers at Geo. A. Hormel & Co. in Austin, Minnesota went on strike for a new contract. They were members of Local P-9, United Food and Commercial Workers (UFCW), AFL-CIO. (The *P* stands for *packinghouse*.) They demanded the restoration of wages and benefits, which the company had cut drastically the previous year. An even more crucial issue was safety.

In the last full year before the strike, the Hormel plant in Austin had one of the highest injury rates in the U.S. meat-packing industry. In that year, there were 202 injuries for every 100 workers in the plant. The national average for all industries was 10 per 100. The meat-packing industry average was 33 per 100. In 1984, fully one third of the workers in the Austin plant suffered injuries serious enough to cause lost time on the job.

In October 1984, Local P-9 members were hit with a 23 percent wage cut, from $10.69 an hour to $8.25. This cost the average worker almost $100 from the weekly paycheck.

Six months later, an arbitrator's ruling put the wage

at $8.75, but allowed the company to cut benefits deeply, including the coverage under the company-carried health insurance plan. These cuts were made retroactive to September 3, 1984.

Workers who, in the meantime, had used the health plan for themselves or members of their families were suddenly in debt to the company for their retroactively not-covered medical and dental bills. In some cases this amounted to thousands of dollars, in others many hundreds. The company deducted this, chunk by chunk, from the already mangled weekly paychecks.

Other benefits, for example the clothing and clothing change allowance, which was eliminated under the new rules, also had to be paid back retroactively.

Some of the cuts had more far-reaching effects than a loss of money. For example, the time allowed for individual workers to sharpen the knives they used was eliminated. Financially, this amounted to less than $5 per week. But henceforth they were to use presharpened knives and not take the time to do it themselves.

Old-timers explain that each person holds and wields a knife slightly differently. By experience they learn the precise sharpening that is most appropriate for them, and the knife becomes shaped to their individual work habit. Presharpened knives, however, are all the same. According to these experts, the incidence of carpal tunnel syndrome—a nerve disease common among Hormel workers, caused by overloading certain muscles of the wrist and hand—will be increased with the use of presharpened knives.

* * *

The Hormel workers were fighting mad. More so because they worked for the country's most profitable pork

6

packer. Their productivity, according to Wall Street analysts, was substantially higher than workers in the rest of the industry.

One reason is that they worked in a modern, state-of-the-art plant that was only two years old. The workers themselves had loaned the company $20 million to help build it.

The new plant, adjacent to the old one on the edge of town, was opened in 1982 while the old one—which had been built in the 1920s—was still being phased out.

In 1975 the company threatened to close down its Austin meat-packing operation. Its main plant had been located there since George A. Hormel founded the company in 1891. Under the threat to build its new flagship plant elsewhere, Hormel forced a major concessionary contract on the local union in 1978. The contract provided:

- that the new plant would be built in Austin.
- that there would be no strikes until three years after the new plant was opened—in effect a seven-year no-strike clause.
- that with few exceptions the past practices from the old plant—where the union traditionally had tight control over working conditions—would not be precedent in the new.
- that production standards would be 20 percent higher at the new plant than at the old.[1]

---

1. According to Jim Guyette, the president of Local P-9 (currently in trusteeship), the company played games with this rise in production standards. The old plant was supposed to have been 20 percent below normal for the industry work pace. The workers were told they would be working 20 percent harder at the new plant.

But at the new plant, unlike the old, production standards were not subject to negotiation; the company set them arbitrarily. After cranking up 20 percent, management added more. Many of the standards, says Guyette, "were never met, it was just impossible." (Which is, incidentally, why so many partially disabled and not-so-young workers "voluntarily" chose to retire early or even quit.)

- that a large part of the incentive pay of workers at the old plant would be put into escrow to provide a $20 million loan to help the company build the $100 million new plant.

This amounted to $12,000 per worker covered by the incentive system. The deal was that the loan would be paid back in weekly amounts added to the basic wage at the new plant and that these payments would continue even after the loan was repaid. Thus workers who received incentive pay at the old plant would be guaranteed substitute-for-incentive pay for as long as they worked at the new plant. This is the arrangement that convinced many of the old-plant workers to accept the 1978 pact. They were told they would never receive less pay than they were earning.

However, the vast majority of the 3,000 old-plant workers were phased out in the transition period from the old to the new. This was accomplished by the layoffs of some 500 workers—most of whom were never rehired—and by attrition, including retirement, transfers to other plants, quits, and so on. Most of the phased-out workers who had contributed to the loan were repaid the amount each had loaned—period. Only around 600 ever became eligible for the substitute-for-incentive pay.

One rationale for accepting this agreement was to save jobs. As it turned out, over the five-year transition period, the 3,000 jobs at the old plant became 1,500 at the new.

By 1985 only some 400 unionized employees who had worked at the old plant were still working for Hormel at the new Austin plant. The balance of the 1,500 had been hired since the new plant opened. These workers would never receive the incentive pay, which averaged around 38 percent over and above the basic wage. In reality then, the 1978 agreement contained a whopping two-tier wage structure, among other concessions.

Pete Winkels and Jim Guyette, then rank and filers (Winkels later became the local business agent), spoke against the 1978 agreement in local meetings on these grounds. They felt the future of the next generation of workers, and therefore of Austin itself, was being traded off.

Guyette's father and grandfather worked at Hormel Austin. Winkels is a fourth generation Hormel worker. Winkels started at the old plant in 1967, Guyette in 1968.

It must be said here that these concessions by Local P-9 were resented by union members at Hormel plants in other parts of the country. It should also be noted that the 1978 agreement was made with the full participation and approval of the officers of the International Union. And that the officers of Local P-9 who negotiated and signed that agreement were not the same as those who were later elected on a program of fighting concessions. The new leadership replaced the old little by little in elections between 1980 and 1985.

It should also be said that the membership of Local P-9 that elected the new leadership was not exactly the same as the rank and file that accepted the 1978 agreement. Eleven hundred people were hired after the new plant opened. But even those who worked at both the old and new plants, who worked throughout the whole seven years, had a change of attitude because of the brutal approach of management in the new plant.

* * *

P-9 did not strike when the company made the 23 percent wage cut in October 1984, because a strike was ruled illegal until the seven-year no-strike clause of the 1978 agreement ran out in August 1985. Besides, the local union was confident it would win the case in arbitration against these mid-term contract cuts. The Local based this expectation on two facts:

First, the summary of a wage-freeze contract that was

negotiated for Hormel workers by UFCW International Union officials in 1981 contained the following language: "The cost-of-living adjustment which is now in effect will be incorporated into the rates, and there will be no increase or reduction in rates for the balance of the present term of the Agreement and for the 1982–1985 term of the Agreement."

Second, an identical case involving the same wage-freeze language in a contract between another UFCW local and the Oscar Mayer Company resulted in the cuts being ruled illegal by the arbitrator.

The summary of the wage-freeze contract had been prepared by UFCW Packinghouse Director Lewie Anderson and distributed to the Local P-9 members before they voted to accept it in 1981. Anderson himself appeared before the Local to explain the contract prior to the balloting. He said it meant no reduction in basic wages. This was presented as one justification for the concessions in the contract, which included loss of the cost-of-living allowance after the first year. This, said Anderson, was a trade-off to prevent the company from cutting the basic wage.

P-9's membership did not see the full text of the contract. They took Anderson's summary as good coin. It wasn't.

In December 1984, as the Local leaders were preparing their case against the October wage cuts, they were informed by the lawyer they had retained, Robert Nichols—who also worked for the UFCW International—that the language protecting wage rates contained in the summary was missing from the full text of the contract. It could not be used in the Local's case before the arbitrator. As a result the arbitrator ruled the company had a right to make wage and benefit cuts.[2]

---

2. The legalities around this case are too complex to describe here. They involve the "me-too clause," a provision carried over into the

Local P-9 President Jim Guyette, who had been elected in December 1983, demanded an explanation from the International Union officials of what had happened to the missing language. It was not forthcoming. Anderson and attorney Nichols said that it was a clerical error.

In February 1985, Local P-9's executive board filed charges with the UFCW against Packinghouse Director Anderson demanding that he explain the missing language. UFCW President William Wynn refused to conduct a hearing on the charges, dismissing them on specious technical grounds. Local P-9 appealed to the International Executive Board, which upheld Wynn's position.

There has never been a satisfactory explanation of what happened to the missing language.

Anderson brazened it out, saying it didn't matter anyway because a summary was never intended to be an accurate description of the full contract.

Guyette says that, beginning in 1981, he repeatedly demanded to see the actual contract. He was always told it was still being worked on by lawyers. "So I told them," he recalls, "to give me whatever you've got." Not until December 1984 did he get to see it.

＊ ＊ ＊

The United Food and Commercial Workers Union, the International Union to which P-9 was affiliated, is relatively

---

1978 agreement as a past practice going back to the 1940 agreement. Traditionally, whatever base rate the larger unionized meat-packing companies settled for, Hormel workers got automatically. From 1940 to 1978 this always meant a raise in the base rate. But by 1984 the International officials had approved so many concessionary contracts in the industry, that the prevailing rate had fallen sharply. Hormel insisted on following suit.

new. It was formed by a merger completed in 1978–79 between the Retail Clerks International Union and the Amalgamated Meat Cutters and Butcher Workmen, which itself had merged with the United Packinghouse Workers of America in 1969.[3]

Local P-9, however, is one of the oldest industrial union locals in the U.S. meat-packing industry. It was organized in 1933 at the Hormel plant and was chartered—or rather it chartered itself—as Local 1 of the Independent Union of All Workers. That year it gained its first pay raise with a three-day sit-down strike. This was the first major sit-down strike of the labor upsurge of the 1930s.

* * *

It seems strange to outsiders, but one of the signs occasionally carried by P-9 strikers declares, "Jay Hormel cared." Jay C. Hormel was the son of the company founder and its chief executive officer from 1929 until his death in 1954.

In the early decades of this century meat packinghouse workers tended to be "boomers," itinerant workers who followed the seasonal rushes in the slaughtering of sheep, cattle, and hogs, and then moved on. They suffered long periods without work when they were forced to take to the road. When they worked, they generally lived in shanties on the edge of town and were not well respected in the community.

The story is told that M.B. Thompson, former Hormel

---

3. The United Food and Commercial Workers has about 1,300,000 members: 800,000 in retail (mostly grocery store employees), 61%; 250,000 in poultry and processing, 19%; 150,000 in other trades (barbers, beauticians, nursing home employees, etc.), 12%; and 100,000 in meat-packing, 8%. (This breakdown is taken from a brochure distributed by the North American Meat Packers Union in July 1986.)

company president, was overheard at the country club complaining that the workers in Austin lived in nice homes. "Before I'm through they'll be living in tar-paper shacks," he is said to have declared. The story is legend now and P-9 demonstrations often feature a tar-paper shack.

Jay Hormel found it difficult to keep skilled meatcutters around Austin to be available when he needed them. To solve this problem he instituted a type of guaranteed annual wage for some workers in the Austin plant, shortly after he took control of the company's operations.

Jay Hormel recognized the union in July 1933, but it took the sit-down strike in November to get a wage increase. Hormel tried to break the strike by appealing to Governor Floyd B. Olson to send in troops. Olson mobilized three hundred Minnesota National Guardsmen in preparation for such a move, but first went to Austin to mediate personally.

Hormel said he wanted to avoid bloodshed. Besides there were several million dollars worth of meat in danger of rotting if the plant's refrigeration was turned off for any length of time. Jay Hormel finally agreed to settle without firing any strikers. The workers got a 10 percent raise. Not much, but the union was firmly established in the plant.

Most of the present-day P-9ers are not old enough to have known Jay Hormel, or to have worked in the old plant when he was in charge of the company. But Austin is a town of only 22,000 and at one time the old plant employed nearly 7,000.

Many families have generations who worked in the plant. The younger people have heard, from friends or relatives who did work there during the "good old days" from 1940 to the mid-1960s, what it was like—or at least what the older folks like to remember about it.

Once Jay Hormel was forced to deal with the union, he

never again tried to break it. Instead he adapted his paternalistic policies to the new situation.

It is said that before the union came in 1933, Jay Hormel used to describe management there as a "benevolent dictatorship." For the workers, however, the dictatorship was a lot more obvious than the benevolence.

By 1936 the union had established firm control over working conditions inside the plant. This was accomplished by struggle, including sit-down stoppages in various departments at different times.

Key to this control was in-plant seniority, where management had to assign jobs or move people from one gang or department to another according to their time in the plant. This broke the onerous system that prevailed until 1933 where foremen tended to be little dictators, imposing personal prejudices and demanding favors—including in some cases sexual favors from women workers—for the better assignments.

Due in part to innovations introduced by Jay Hormel and in part to the in-plant strength of the union, the following situation evolved between 1933 and 1940:

Most of the workers had a guarantee of fifty-two straight-time, flat-rate paychecks per year regardless of the hours worked. A fifty-two-week layoff notice was required.

If a gang completed its quota of work early, its members could decide among themselves to go home or continue work and be paid the extra money. This in turn evolved into an incentive system under which the workers themselves, in different departments and gangs, collectively determined the pace of work, or speed of the line, and received extra pay for production over the standard. The standards were not set arbitrarily by the company but through negotiations.

Shop-floor disputes were generally settled on the spot

by negotiations between management and the workers directly involved.

In 1940 the company and the union signed a Permanent Working Agreement, without an expiration date, which included setting the basic wage rate at the level of the old "Big Four" packing companies—Armour, Swift, Wilson, and Cudahy.

Under this system the employees at Austin Hormel were the highest paid workers in the packinghouse industry on an annual basis. They also generally worked fewer hours. What is more, as the old-timers will testify, they worked very hard, but they worked with dignity, since they set their own pace and could take breaks when they needed them.

The 1940 agreement lasted twenty-eight years. According to a brief history of the Local prepared by its officers after the strike began in August 1985:

"The relationship between the company and Local 9 began to deteriorate after the death of Jay Hormel in 1954. A new group of managers from Nebraska, led by company president M.B. Thompson, took over operation of the Hormel company. They had little allegiance to the town where the company was born, and began to acquire plants in other places while tightening controls over the Austin facility. This new management first forced concessions in 1963 . . . and in 1978 made the union (now P-9) give up the incentive system and production bonuses."

In fourteen of the twenty years between 1963 and 1983, significant concessions were demanded by the company and accepted by the union. These included such items as the company threatening in 1974 to close the beef kill operation unless the workers involved took a $30 per week cut. They made the concession, but in 1975 the beef kill was eliminated anyway.

The new-plant agreement did continue the guaranteed

Local P-9 Executive members. Above, left to right: Lynn Huston (vice-president), Jim Guyette (president) and James Retterath. Below: Kathy Buck (financial secretary) with striking wood-workers in the state of Washington,

annual wage, the fifty-two-week layoff notice, and the crucial in-plant seniority system.

When the new plant was opened, however, it became clear that management no longer accepted the enforcement of the seniority system as a matter of course. What is more, without the old incentive system the foremen once again had the responsibility of staying on the workers to get out production.

According to Jim Guyette: "The ratio of supervisors to workers was all out of proportion. In some places there was one foreman for every three workers." Workers' control of the speed of the line had been lost, along with the all-important dignity. Workers now even had to raise their hands to get permission to go to the toilet—something they didn't have to do at the old plant.

* * *

In the meantime drastic changes were taking place within the entire meat-packing industry. In part this resulted from an economic pinch with beef and pork consumption declining from 1979 to 1982. But the changes were also part of the nationwide employer offensive against working people, which has been unfolding since the mid-1970s.

The larger packinghouse companies, including the old "Big Four," suffered crises. Mergers and acquisitions by conglomerates took place, sometimes involving the draining of finances from the packing companies. According to Jim Guyette:

"A sharply rising monopolization of the market resulted in plant closings, Chapter 11 bankruptcies, and layoffs. . . .

"Virtually alone among the major packinghouses, the Hormel Company remained a highly profitable enterprise and was characterized by Business Week in 1984 as the 'envy of the industry.' Nevertheless Hormel seized upon the crisis in the industry as an opportunity to drive down the wages and benefits of its workers."[4]

In the face of the crisis in the industry—a crisis largely created by finance capital—the International Union developed a policy of "controlled retrenchment." The term appears in the UFCW Packinghouse Division report of March 1984. The terms "controlled retreat" and "controlled concessions" are also used to mean the same thing. According to the April 15, 1985, *Business Week*: "Since December, 1980, the union has been on what UFCW President William H. Wynn calls a 'controlled retreat.' Wages in pork packing have fallen by as much as 40% below the 1980 wage of $10.69 an hour."

This policy was applied to the profitable Hormel Company as well to those companies crying bankruptcy. The 1981 contract giving up the cost-of-living allowance was part of this policy.

Guyette, who had been on the Local's executive board only since 1980, opposed accepting the 1981 wage-freeze package on the ground that "further concessions should not be offered to the industry's most profitable employer." It seemed to a growing number of P-9 workers that an uncontrolled rout—not a controlled retreat—was going to be the result of further concessions.

A majority of the executive board recommended that the wage-freeze proposal be accepted. Guyette made a minority report, which was voted up by the membership. Later, the local membership voted to reject the wage-freeze proposal. UFCW Packinghouse Director Lewie Anderson then insisted on a second vote. This time he put it forward as a vote to remain within the Hormel "chain."

---

4. May 16, 1986, Guyette affidavit.

The chain was supposed to be a unified bargaining procedure involving meetings of representatives of all the locals organizing workers in Hormel plants. The International Union officials interpreted a vote to remain within the chain as a vote in favor of the concessionary contract. This time the proposal passed, with Guyette making an unsuccessful challenge of the balloting procedure.

When this contract went into effect in 1982, the basic rate of pay was supposed to be frozen at $10.69 per hour until 1985. This rate applied to the entire Hormel chain. A wage reopener would come due September 1, 1984, with a right to strike. This was presented at the time as giving the locals a chance to gain a wage increase in 1984.

But when 1984 came around the Hormel company was demanding further cuts in wages and benefits. Hormel's argument was based not on lack of profits but solely on the ground that its basic wage rate was now higher than rates prevailing in the rest of the industry. The fact that its productivity and profits were also much higher was irrelevant, according to the company.

The officers of the International Union were not ignorant of some of the measures necessary to make a serious fight against the cutback drive. They even put them in writing from time to time. They just didn't implement them.

For example, the UFCW Packinghouse Division's policy statements of 1983, 1984, and 1985 outlined guidelines for local unions to follow in responding to company demands for concessions. These included:

• Locals should refuse to make midterm contract concessions.

• Concessions should be granted an employer only as a last resort and only after bitter struggle.

• Concessions should not be made to profitable companies under any circumstances.

• Locals within each chain should seek to establish common expiration dates for their contracts. (Common expiration dates for contracts allow the union to threaten a strike at the same time at all the company's facilities and prevent the company from using concessions, dragged from one local, in negotiations with others.)

• The right of workers in one local to refuse to cross picket lines established by other locals on strike should be protected and extended.

These principles, if implemented, would have strengthened the ability of the locals to resist concessions. These principles were reiterated at the meetings of locals in the Hormel chain held in Chicago in the spring of 1984.

But immediately thereafter, Packinghouse Director Anderson approved separate negotiations by Ottumwa Local 431, in Iowa, in response to company demands for large cuts in wages, benefits, and incentive bonuses. The other locals in the chain were not even consulted. They learned about it from the news media.

The Ottumwa workers faced a vicious company offensive. When the local voted down the concessions, the company laid off 444 workers, shutting down its cut and kill (boning and slaughtering) operations. It declared the layoffs would be permanent and the plant would be closed if the concessions were not accepted. Another vote was called and the result was the same. The next day the company laid off an additional 114 workers repeating its threat to close the plant. The International Union officials simply left the Ottumwa workers to face this pressure alone. By a slim majority, Ottumwa Local 431 members then accepted the 23 percent wage-and-benefit cut. When the elimination of bonuses was included, it came to over 30 percent.

"Ottumwa Local 431" is actually a unit of what is known in the UFCW as a District Local Union (sometimes called an amalgamated local). District Local Union 431 has some 8,000 members in many units spread over a large area. It includes units of retail clerks and many other kinds of workers. Each unit has no autonomy and can make no major decisions without approval of the District Local Union. In effect this means approval by its top official, since the Local has general membership meetings only once a year. The head of Local 431 is its secretary-treasurer and business manager, Louis DeFrieze, who approved the concessionary contract for the Ottumwa plant and gave "Ottumwa 431" no help in resisting company demands.

The new base wage at Ottumwa was down from $10.69 to $8.75 an hour (with a raise in September to $9 and a year later to $10). The solidarity of the chain had been broken at Ottumwa with the approval of the International Union officials. The anti-concession guidelines turned out to be empty ritual. The company had been allowed to pick off one local in isolation.

What is more, the expiration date on the Ottumwa contract was May 1987, putting it out of sync with the rest of the chain and in particular with Fremont, Nebraska, and Austin, the other two plants with slaughtering operations. (As far as the Hormel chain is concerned, common expiration dates at these three plants are key because they supply raw meat to the other facilities.)

Before the Ottumwa contract was signed, Jim Guyette sharply protested this violation of the guidelines in three letters to UFCW President William Wynn, to no avail.

* * *

At the subsequent chain meetings in July 1984, Anderson reiterated his philosophy that concessions were inevitable. He proposed the Hormel chain accept the Ottumwa pattern to avoid even worse cuts the company would make unilaterally.

According to Guyette, "I, again, advanced the argument that, with respect to a highly profitable company such as Hormel, we should be discussing wage increases, not concessions. I asked Anderson once again to tell us what his program was for fighting back against the company's demands for concessions.

"Anderson responded to me by stating that if I genuinely believed in fighting concessions, then I should 'guarantee' that Local P-9 would go out on strike in September, 'legal or illegal.' He further stated, much to my surprise, that the Hormel Company was going to take the position that a strike by P-9 in September would be illegal. . . .

"I replied that, as Anderson well knew, I could hardly 'guarantee' that P-9 would strike in September, when no strike vote had as yet been even proposed, let alone passed upon by the requisite two-thirds majority mandated by the UFCW constitution. Second, I told Anderson that if, in fact, his claim that such a strike might be illegal was true, it was even more preposterous to expect me to 'guarantee' on the spot that the membership of my local would vote to strike. I did, however, assure him that we would promptly determine whether we were legally entitled to strike in September, take a strike vote, and, in any case, do everything in our power to support any strike action taken by the chain."[5]

Local P-9 submitted the matter to expedited arbitration, and the arbitrator found that P-9 did not have the right to strike in September 1984 but would have to wait until August 1985.

This is the way a publication of the UFCW International

---

5. May 16, 1986, Guyette affidavit.

Union describes the same incident: "All the locals except Local P-9 agreed in July to strike Hormel in September if the chain could not reach an agreement. Local P-9's president, Jim Guyette, expressed concern about the local's legal right to strike in light of the no-strike clause in their contract [stemming from 1978] and questioned whether the local's members would support a strike by the other Hormel workers."

Clearly Anderson's question to Guyette was a setup designed to provide an argument for shifting the blame for breaking the chain onto Local P-9. In all the many statements to this effect issued by the International officers both before and after the P-9 strike began in August 1985, there is no mention of the fact that it was the Ottumwa agreement of May 1984 that actually broke the chain, with the approval of Lewie Anderson.

There was no strike by the other members of the chain in September 1984. Instead, at chain meetings from which P-9 had been excluded it was agreed to accept contracts on the Ottumwa pattern, including the $1.69 cut in wages.

What is more, these agreements provided that the Fremont contract would expire in September 1986. Thus the three expiration dates of the slaughtering plants were entirely out of sync: Austin, August 1985; Fremont, September 1986; and Ottumwa, May 1987.

* * *

In 1985 the International Union sent out a table listing the UFCW-organized slaughtering plants as well as the expiration dates for each contract. It was reproduced in the January 2, 1986, issue of P-9's newspaper, The Unionist. Pete Winkels, who took office in 1985 as P-9's business agent, commented:

Local P-9 Executive members. Above, left to right: Pete Winkels (business agent), Carl Pontius, Floyd Lenoch. Below, left: John "Skinny" Weis. Below, right: Ray Rogers, codirector of Corporate Campaign, Inc.

"Local P-9 has been told many times by Mr. Lewie Anderson that 'you have no overview.' . . . This is the 'overview' that Lewie Anderson says we are lacking. You don't need a weatherman to tell you it's raining and you don't need an International Vice President to explain his program, in terms of success. All you have to do is be able to read. . . .

"Never have I ever seen such difference in expiration dates in this industry. My experience goes back only to 1967, yet I remember then that all contracts came due at once. Since Lewie took over in 1979 as head of packing, we now have expiration dates scattered to the point that there is no common expiration dates for any of the chains. This problem is not unique to Hormel. Not only are the years scattered, but also the months of the years in which these contracts come due.

"If I headed a corporation or lending institution doing business with these companies, I would view these expiration dates with glee. How much better, or easier, to defeat somebody than to weaken them by dividing the unity, or power, they have. Packinghouse workers do not need a program that allows for individual plants to be isolated and picked off one at a time. I don't want anyone to think that I blame Lewie Anderson for all the troubles that exist in our industry. . . . [But] having an 'overview' does not make up for being incompetent."[6]

* * *

In the lobby of the Labor Center in Austin, Minnesota, there hangs a picture of an elderly man, with a brass plate

---

6. Back in 1933, the union member who escorted Jay Hormel out of the plant as the sit-down strike began was John Winkels, Pete's uncle. John is now a retired P-9 member. Pete's father, Casper, is also a retired P-9 member.

beneath it that reads: "Frank Ellis, founder of the Austin Labor Movement."

Ellis started work as a young boy helping his father on the killing floor of the Swift plant in St. Louis, Missouri. After participating in a strike in 1904 he ran away from home and soon joined the Industrial Workers of the World (IWW), the class-struggle oriented union founded in Chicago in 1905.

At that time, most unions affiliated with the American Federation of Labor (AFL) were craft unions. They organized only the skilled workers and ignored the unskilled and semiskilled—the bulk of the production workers in industry. With few exceptions they catered to the racism of the employers, and they largely refused to organize women workers. To make matters worse, each separate craft union organized only its particular craft. A factory that was "successfully" organized by the AFL craft unions in those days might have a dozen different unions, with a dozen different contracts, and a dozen expiration dates, and still leave the bulk of the workers in the plant unorganized.

The IWW started out with the idea of organizing all workers into one big union with different branches for different industries. The IWW got sidetracked along the way and failed in its stated objective. By the 1930s it was more a legend than a living movement.

But for fifteen years or so, the Wobblies—as the IWW activists were called—did a lot of organizing and led some effective strikes using mass picketing and protest demonstrations. And they spread the ideas of industrial unionism among tens of thousands of young workers, many of whom would later participate in the rise of the CIO—the Congress of Industrial Organizations.

Frank Ellis absorbed these ideas and talked them up on the various jobs he held in packinghouses across the Midwest. He became a highly skilled butcher and an effective on-the-job union organizer.

For a while he was president of an Amalgamated Meat Cutters local at the Wilson plant in Oklahoma City but soon moved on. The Amalgamated was an AFL craft union, and Ellis had industrial unionism in his heart.

In 1928, Ellis, now in his thirties, was hired at the Austin Hormel plant to set up a casings processing department. While a foreman he got jobs for other union-conscious workers. By 1933 he had connections throughout the plant. Among them were Joe Ollman, an Austin native who worked on the hog kill gang, and Joe Voorhees, later business agent for the local.

In July of that year a brief work stoppage in the hog kill precipitated a series of large public meetings at which the Independent Union of All Workers (IUAW), led by Frank Ellis, was organized.

In November came the sit-down strike, during part of which Ellis and Jay Hormel stood on tables outside the plant debating the issues before the strikers.

Once the union was established in the Hormel plant the IUAW used this base to spread unionism in the area.

In Austin and in the nearby Minnesota town of Albert Lea, the IUAW organized workers in restaurants, hotels, garages, retail stores, taverns, lumberyards, and many small factories. This expansion was sparked by Eva Sauer, a clerk who became a full-time IUAW organizer in 1934. Several strikes were key to this. Demonstrations, consumer boycotts, and other activities were also used to bring pressure on the employers. All this was backed up by the massive presence of union members from the Hormel plant if necessary. By 1940 Austin was a virtually solid union town.

Organizers from the Austin IUAW also traveled to packing plants throughout Minnesota, the Dakotas, and Iowa.

There are those who say that Jay Hormel was not opposed to this on the ground that if he had to meet union wages and conditions, then so should his competitors.

Eventually IUAW locals existed as far northwest as Fargo, North Dakota, and as far south as Ottumwa, Iowa.

In the mid-1930s the events around Austin, Minnesota, were not that exceptional. Mass production workers here and there across the country were beginning to organize in spite of the refusal of the AFL tops to help them. In 1934 there were even three citywide general strikes that succeeded in organizing the San Francisco longshoremen, the Toledo Auto-Lite workers, and the truck drivers and warehousemen in Minneapolis.

Ellis worked with the leaders of the Minneapolis Teamsters in regional organizing. One of them was Farrell Dobbs, who later commented in his book *Teamster Power:*

"The central leader of the IUAW was Frank Ellis, a man with considerable experience in the IWW. Although not a Marxist, he had absorbed many class-struggle concepts, and he was every inch a fighter. He did all he could to teach the workers that they must rely entirely on their own strength, never putting their trust in any agent of the capitalist class. Ellis warned especially against thinking the workers could get any justice in the capitalist courts."

At the 1935 convention of the AFL, the question of organizing workers into industrial unions in the mass production industries finally came to the fore. The majority of AFL officials still opposed the idea, but a minority, headed by John L. Lewis, decided to proceed. (Lewis' United Mine Workers union was an exception among AFL-affiliated international unions. It was already an industrial union that traditionally tried to organize all workers in the coal mines, regardless of craft or skill.) After the convention, Lewis and leaders of a few other AFL unions formed a Committee for

Industrial Organization (CIO) within the AFL.

Shortly thereafter, Joe Voorhees wrote to Lewis on behalf of the IUAW. But the IUAW was not in the AFL and the CIO still was, and Lewis was noncommittal. Only after the CIO was expelled from the AFL in 1936, and after the Amalgamated Meat Cutters voted in May 1937 to stay with the AFL, did the CIO give its endorsement to the IUAW and other independent unions in the packinghouse industry. Later that month the Austin local voted to affiliate with the CIO, by then called the Congress of Industrial Organizations. The other IUAW locals followed.

In their area, the IUAW locals formed the backbone of the Packinghouse Workers Organizing Committee (PWOC), which was set up by the CIO later that year.

PWOC organizers from Austin ranged north to the major packinghouses of South St. Paul and south into Iowa, their expenses paid by contributions from the Austin Hormel workers. In 1943 the United Packinghouse Workers of America (UPWA) was finally chartered by the CIO as an autonomous international union.

The structure of the UPWA-CIO included ten regional directors who were elected within the region and could not be removed by the International. Frank Ellis was elected vice president of the new union. Joe Ollman became the first director of the region in which Austin was located.

The Austin local, now called Local 9, UPWA-CIO, was no longer the center of union power in the region, however. Numerically the Austin plant was dwarfed by the then much larger packinghouses in South St. Paul and elsewhere.

The Permanent Working Agreement and its provision for setting the basic wage rate on the pattern of the "Big Four" worked out so that strikes did not occur at the Austin plant. Instead, Hormel workers were generous in their support of strikers at other packinghouses. This included not only hundreds of thousands of dollars but carloads of pickets when the going got rough.

Throughout the current struggle of Local P-9, one of the strongest and most consistent groups of supporters have been the retired members. They have pitched in on almost every task and done so in remarkably large numbers. Not the least of their contributions has been to help resurrect this history from their memories in story after story on the picket line or around the union hall, providing a living continuity with the younger generation.

* * *

By the time the Ottumwa local was being picked off by Hormel in the spring of 1984, it was reasonably clear to P-9ers that unless they were just going to lie down and accept the concessions demanded by the company, they had better prepare to fight. The company had already hired a notorious union-busting specialist, the Milwaukee law firm of Krukowski, Chet, Beck and Loomis.

In April a membership meeting passed a motion instructing the Local P-9 Executive Board to ask the International Union for help in formulating a publicity campaign to fight concessions. On April 30, 1984, Guyette wrote to UFCW President Wynn about this. On May 8 Wynn replied that the International Union was already doing what it could in this regard and he saw no need to expand these efforts.

Guyette took the idea of the Local hiring a public relations expert to the P-9 Executive Board and was authorized to look for one. He searched the Twin Cities and elsewhere and couldn't find one who would work for the union. Then he noticed an article in *Business Week* that mentioned Ray Rogers and his New York-based Corporate Campaign, Inc. (CCI). Rogers had developed the corporate campaign concept and directed the first such effort as part of the fight to force J.P. Stevens to deal with the textile workers' union in a number of its southern plants.

Guyette called Rogers, who explained that the Corporate Campaign was not a public relations service. The idea was to research and expose the financial interests behind the company's antiunion decisions and to activate the union members and sympathizers on the broadest scale possible to increase the union's power and bring it to bear.

Rogers was brought briefly to Austin to present the idea to the members of the P-9 Executive Board. They liked it and decided to propose it at the next meeting of the Hormel chain. There Lewie Anderson opposed it, and the majority of the local board changed their minds.

By that time the company was making it plain it would shortly impose large wage cuts at Austin.

Lynn Huston, then a rank and filer whose father had forty-three years in the plant, drew up and circulated a petition for a special meeting of Local P-9 to consider a motion to invite Rogers and CCI codirector Ed Allen to make a presentation to the membership. Huston had no trouble getting the necessary signatures. The meeting was held and the motion passed overwhelmingly. It was the membership of Local P-9 that brought in Rogers and that has voted on and controlled CCI's activities throughout.

Before Rogers came to Austin, Guyette again sought approval and cooperation from UFCW Packinghouse Director Lewie Anderson, who referred him to President William Wynn. Wynn said he would consider the proposal to hire Rogers.

Shortly thereafter, Wynn sent the following mailgram to Rogers: "We are informed that you are discussing a 'corporate campaign' with UFCW Local 9 against the George A. Hormel and Company. The Austin, Minnesota Local is only one of the UFCW Locals that represent employees at Hormel. The other locals have not assented to a campaign, nor has the International sanctioned any such effort. Our Packinghouse Division is directed by Vice President Lewie Anderson. Any campaign that is initiated without his involvement and the approval of the affected locals and the International would be very regrettable."

Guyette once again sought approval, first by going to see UFCW Region 13 Director Wendell Olson and his assistant Joseph T. Hansen. Guyette was accompanied by Floyd Lenoch, a member of the P-9 Executive Board who had over thirty years in the plants, both old and new.[7] Another meeting was arranged for the top UFCW officers to talk to Guyette and Lynn Huston together with Ray Rogers and Ed Allen.

Again Wynn said the campaign would be considered. A meeting was arranged for Guyette and Rogers to make a presentation before representatives of locals in the chain. The response was good. But the campaign was never put to a vote of these locals.

Instead, the International officials announced their disapproval immediately after a December 20, 1984, meeting of the UFCW Packinghouse Committee, where Rogers and Guyette were given all of thirty minutes for their presentation. It was a cut-and-dried decision already made beforehand. Material denouncing the campaign was ready for distribution to the press as the meeting ended.

---

7. Floyd Lenoch, whose father also had worked in the plant, is well respected both for his experience and tact. He had served on the Local's Executive Board a number of times over the years. During negotiations over the 1978 Agreement, he had been the lone dissenting voice on the board. He was elected president of Local P-9 in 1980, but chose not to run for the post in 1983, when Jim Guyette was elected. He ran for Executive Board instead and was elected.

The International Union officialdom counterposed a campaign against the ConAgra conglomerate to P-9's proposal for one against Hormel. (Packinghouse Director Anderson referred to the projected effort as "a full-court press.") ConAgra had purchased the Armour company, shut down most of its plants, then reopened them nonunion with wage rates in the $6 per hour range. The ConAgra-Armour campaign was never seriously developed, however. The UFCW lost a National Labor Relations Board election at those plants.

Meanwhile, through its research, the Corporate Campaign, Inc. had discovered that First Bank, which has interlocking directorates and major stock and credit relationships with Hormel, also is connected to ConAgra. CCI proposed the UFCW combine the campaigns.

According to Guyette, he and Rogers also proposed a two-pronged program for the meat-packing industry: (1) Stabilize the wage rates at the higher paying companies such as Hormel; (2) Bring up the wages at the lower paying companies. This, they said, would begin to solve the problem of organizing the nonunion plants. "You can't expect," says Guyette, "to get workers to join the union, or even to vote for it in certification elections, if they aren't going to make any more paying union dues, than remaining nonunion."

In the meantime, shortly after the 23 percent wage cut in October 1984, Rogers spoke before a meeting in Austin of several thousand P-9 members and their families.

At this meeting Rogers explained that recent experience had shown that what had become the traditional methods of strike and boycott were no longer effective. That is, where an employer is put on the AFL-CIO's unfair list, the workers on strike are left alone to wait out the company, and not much else is done. Said Rogers: "We are going to

Above, left: Jan Butts, president of the United Support Group. Above, right: Larry Bastain, recording secretary of United Auto Workers Local 325 at Ford St. Louis, speaking at May 10, 1986, rally in Ottumwa, Iowa. Below: Austin-area farmers demonstrate support for striking meat-packers.

collectively organize your knowledge, skills, imagination, and energies and transform your union into a powerful economic and political force by that mobilization."

Later, after the strike had been on for five months, Lewie Anderson prepared a large packet entitled *Fact Book on Local P-9/Hormel, Austin, MN*. In it he paraphrased Rogers's statement as follows: "Rogers said strikes and boycotts are outdated and ineffective. Moreover, his strategy is far superior. Rogers has now had the Hormel Austin workers on strike for over five months and he is now calling for a boycott."

In January 1985 members of Local P-9 voted to assess themselves $3 a week to finance the campaign. The vote had to be taken again twice because the International tried to get it reversed. The results were the same each time.

The campaign included door-to-door canvassing in towns with meat-packing plants and sending delegations of P-9ers to other local unions and farm groups in a wide area of the Midwest.

It included distribution of special editions of the union newspaper door-to-door in Austin, leafletting and carrying banners at branches of First Bank, which has close ties to Hormel, and sending delegations of P-9ers to the annual stockholders' meetings of First Bank, as well as to a meeting of the Hormel company—the first held outside of Austin (in Atlanta, Georgia) in history.

There was reason enough to expose the First Bank-Hormel connection, but this activity also provided a focus for having demonstrations while the P-9 members were still working.

In all these activities, P-9 members, supporters, retirees, and families were drawn in, gaining experience and confidence.

P-9 and the CCI had some hope of forcing the company

to sign a decent contract without a strike, but they certainly didn't count on it. Preparations for a strike were organized systematically, including refurbishing the union hall to provide a large kitchen and dining room and space for the distribution of food and clothing.

* * *

In early August 1985, the company made its final contract offer. It was so bad even the UFCW officials recommended rejection and promised the International's full support if P-9 turned down the contract. It did. The Local then requested that the International sanction a strike, and this was granted by telegram August 9. But the same telegram attacked P-9 and placed restrictions on the right to strike. It declared:

"Local 9, contrary to the counsel of the International Union, the Hormel Chain, and the National Packinghouse Committee has broken with the Chain and pursued an independent and isolated course.

"These decisions were made by the Local Union, presumably with the knowledge that in breaching solidarity they could not expect it."

The telegram also excluded permission for a boycott or for extension of picket lines to other plants outside Austin.

On August 16, one day before the strike began, the International Union officials released a position paper to the press again attacking P-9, accusing the Local of breaking the chain and of refusing to go on strike in the fall of 1984, and claiming the Local was "nearly bankrupt" from paying fees to the CCI, which was not true.

The fact is, CCI's fee was $40,000 for the initial research, preparation, and activity from October 1984 to

January 1985, and $20,000 per month from then on, with a $200,000 bonus if the company were forced to return the wage and benefit cuts. Actually CCI was paid only a total of $116,000. After the strike started, CCI declined further fees. It has helped the Local raise more than a million dollars. In effect the CCI—for the present at least—has become indistinguishable from the general support work for the P-9 fight.

As soon as the strike started, the Local and its supporters set in motion a number of democratic committees and procedures to involve all the P-9 members. The United Support Group, which had been formed earlier by spouses of P-9 members, stepped up its activities.

No member who wanted to participate, both in activity and decision making, was left out. This has greatly strengthened the struggle and kept the members well informed. The International Union and UFCW Region 13 provided a total of $65 per week strike benefit, soon cut to $40. But the strikers were able to survive through their own efforts and solidarity from supporters.

A kitchen was set up to feed pickets as well as volunteers around the hall. A food shelf and clothing closet, stocked by donations, provided necessities to strikers and their families. Every once in a while a truck pulled into the parking lot of the Austin Labor Center, from a farm group, another packinghouse union local, or other supporter, to unload bags of potatoes, canned goods, and other food. Throughout the struggle, no strikers or their family members have had to go hungry, though the fare has been light on meat and other expensive items.

P-9 established the Tool Box, a support program to help with emergencies and the stress of the struggle; a War Room, to coordinate the various activities of the Local, including picketing; a Communications Committee, which organizes P-9 members to travel across the country, telling the truth about their fight to unions and other organizations and appealing for aid.

An "Adopt A P-9 Family Fund" was set up to deal with things like the threatened loss of a home, eviction from an apartment, threatened loss of a car sorely needed for transportation, or exceptional medical expenses. Things like boats and extra cars were not covered by this program, and some went by the board. In November 1985 a 50,000 piece mailing was sent out asking unions to contribute to the Adopt A P-9 Family Fund.

* * *

According to Guyette, "In the fall of 1985 the rank and file of Local P-9 voted to extend their picket lines to places performing struck work and to support any local union members honoring our roving picket lines."[8] The members of Ottumwa Local 431, Fremont Local 22, and Dubuque, Iowa, Local 150A pledged to honor P-9's lines. They each also asked the International Union to sanction P-9's extended pickets, as well as a national boycott of Hormel products.

At a meeting of the Hormel chain in early November 1985, the officers of almost all the locals asked the International to sanction extension of the picket lines.

UFCW President Wynn then agreed to issue a joint statement with Guyette saying the International would sanction extension of the picket lines if Hormel did not bargain in good faith.

On November 15, however, Wynn told the press, the company, and P-9 that:

---

8. May 16, 1986, Guyette affidavit.

"No sanction has been granted to extend picket lines . . . and that we will evaluate reports from our representatives as to the good faith evinced by both the company and the Local. . . . Unless and until we sanction an extension our members outside Austin would be taking serious risks and the local unions could be faced with costly and risky litigation if they respected extended picketing. . . ."

"Roving pickets" are an old and solid tradition in the packinghouse industry, however. The right to follow struck work (where the plant on strike has the work done elsewhere) was defended by the old United Packinghouse Workers of America, as well as the Amalgamated Meatcutters' Packinghouse Division. The very idea that the International Union officials have some sort of right to prohibit this is only as old as the UFCW.

* * *

In late December a federal mediator presented a proposed contract that the company accepted. It was essentially the same as the company offer that had precipitated the strike. It left safety entirely up to the judgment of the company, gutted the seniority system, and prohibited handbilling and other constitutionally guaranteed union and political activity by employees. It contained a similar wage to that forced on the rest of the chain. (In January 1986, the annual cash compensation for Hormel Chairman Richard L. Knowlton was increased by $231,000 to $570,000.)

The contract eliminated the guaranteed annual wage and the fifty-two-week layoff notice. It had an expiration date of 1988, which once again put the three slaughtering houses out of sync. Fremont's contract would expire in 1986, Ottumwa's in 1987, and Austin's in 1988.

The UFCW officialdom recommended—or rather in-

Above: Mural on Austin Labor Center dedicated by Local P-9 to jailed anti-apartheid leader Nelson Mandela, May 27, 1986. Banner in mural is inscribed, "If blood be the price of your cursed wealth, good God, we have paid in full," from a poem written by an unknown worker around 1908. Below: Austin police attack a peaceful picket line in April 1986.

sisted—that P-9 accept the mediator's proposal, and that a mail-in ballot be conducted by the International. Instead, Local P-9 held an open meeting on December 21 to discuss the contract and prepare for a vote the following week. In a secret ballot, the membership rejected the mediator's proposal by better than two to one. The International officials challenged the vote, demanding the mail-in ballot. This was held and the contract was again rejected.

On January 13, 1986, Hormel opened the plant to scabs, though not many got past the pickets and mass demonstrations by P-9 supporters.

While local police and deputies under the command of Mower County Sheriff Wayne Goodnature tried to break up the picket lines, UFCW President Wynn sent a message to P-9 President Guyette. Wynn refused to sanction roving pickets or the Hormel boycott, declaring: "Boycotting Hormel products produced under the chain agreement, which has some of the best wages and conditions in the industry, would undermine union jobs paying base labor rates of $10 an hour simply to try to secure the $10.69 an hour in Austin that you have unsuccessfully fought for for 13 months." He insisted Guyette "lead them back to work. . . ."

＊　＊　＊

Thus Wynn helped set the stage for Hormel's next move: getting Democratic-Farmer-Labor Governor Rudy Perpich to send in the Minnesota National Guard.

On January 20, 1986, the Guardsmen arrived in Austin, and by January 23 they were escorting the scabs—mostly nonunion labor—through the picket line.

On January 26, P-9 called for a national boycott of Hormel products. The next day, the Local sent its roving pickets to other plants in the Hormel chain, including Ottumwa and Fremont.

At Ottumwa the great majority of the 750 workers refused to cross the picket lines. (The old leadership of the Ottumwa 431 unit, which had been replaced in the election following the signing of the Ottumwa concession contract, crossed.)

Hormel fired some 500 workers at the Ottumwa plant and has "permanently replaced" 27 at Fremont on the grounds that they were "sympathy strikers." The cut and kill operations at Ottumwa were shut down and have remained closed.

The International Union officials sent representatives to the various Hormel plants to urge workers not to respect P-9's picket lines.

Ten days after the National Guard was sent to Austin and three days after the P-9 pickets were extended to other Hormel plants, UFCW President Wynn sent a telegram to the locals in the Hormel chain. It declared in part: "Rogers has anointed himself the Ayatollah of Austin and is making hostages of our members at other Hormel plants."

P-9 looked at it differently. The Local was giving union members at other plants a chance to join the fight. It was the P-9 membership that made the decision to extend picketing, not Rogers. He was not a member.

The Fremont workers who lost their jobs were able to qualify for unemployment compensation, but initially this was denied to the Ottumwa workers. Neither did they receive strike benefits. At first they had to depend on donations of food and money raised by their own support group, which was initiated by four wives of fired workers. Corporate Campaign, Inc. helped their fund-raising efforts.

On February 21, P-9 removed its pickets from the Ottumwa plant at the request of the fired workers. Immediately thereafter the 500 fired workers marched to the plant gate to report for work. They found the gates chained and padlocked in spite of the promise by Local 431 Business Manager Louis DeFrieze that they would be rehired.

The Iowa authorities, however, did subsequently rule that the locked-out workers were eligible for unemployment benefits. The firings themselves were appealed under a clause in the Ottumwa contract protecting the right of workers to honor an authorized picket line.

* * *

Meanwhile, the presence of the National Guard in Austin, combined with large-scale arrests and an injunction limiting pickets, allowed the company to employ hundreds of scabs and to operate the plant, although on a reduced basis. By February 26 the Austin plant was slaughtering 2,300 hogs a day compared to its normal operating rate of 6,000 a day.

On the other hand, the role of the National Guard made the P-9 strike front-page and prime-time news across the country. Millions of workers became aware of it for the first time. The natural reaction of unionists was to sympathize with the P-9 strikers and to consider the use of the Guard for strikebreaking to be a threat to the entire labor movement. P-9's support work became even more effective than before.

* * *

Less than a week after the Guard arrived in Austin, three hundred Twin Cities union members marched on the Governor's mansion in St. Paul to demand withdrawal of the troops. On January 29, 1986, a rally of 1,000 took place in Ottumwa in support of the fired workers.

On February 4, a P-9 support group was formed in New York; it issued a statement signed by forty-eight union officials and promised to send a delegation to Austin. On February 15, a rally of 3,000 took place in Austin attended by thirty New York labor officials and 300 union representatives from around the country. Later, on March 14, the New York support committee organized a rally of 1,000 and pledged to adopt 100 P-9 families.

Instead of becoming isolated, the P-9 struggle had become a center of labor attention and support nationally. This was due not simply to the widespread publicity, but to the efforts of the strikers themselves. Dozens of members of P-9 and some fired workers from Ottumwa and Fremont traveled around the country to speak to hundreds of union locals.

Wherever they were able to reach the rank and file, they received enthusiastic support from workers who were grateful to find that somewhere unionists were putting up a serious fight against the effort of the corporations and government to drive down the standard of living of U.S. workers.

In response, the UFCW International officers stepped up their attacks on P-9 and did everything they could to undercut the support. For example, on March 4, 1986, International Association of Machinists Lodge 780 sent a letter to UFCW President Wynn enclosing a $10,000 check for the Adopt A P-9 Family Fund. Wynn returned the check to the IAM local in a March 14 letter which said:

"If, despite our request that contributions to support P-9's replaced strikers be sent to our Region for direct distribution to members and not to Local P-9/Corporate Campaign's Adopt a Family Fund, you wish to act contrary to our request, please do it yourself. Also, next time you want to stick it to the UFCW, please don't ask us to bend over and cooperate."

The UFCW headquarters put out a special sixteen-page document dated February 1986 that was sent to AFL-CIO officials nationally. It was entitled: "Special Report: UFCW Local P-9 Strikes Hormel: The International Union's Perspective." It declared:

"Hormel, while a tough bargainer, has not rejected good faith collective bargaining."

It repeated the accusation that P-9 had broken with the Hormel chain and blamed Ray Rogers for firing up the P-9 rank-and-file into an unreasonable state of mind. It also contained the following scurrilous passage:

"Objectively, the quality of organization and communications that the corporate campaign generated must be recognized. It fully exploited the real grievances of the Austin members, though not with an accurate overview of the situation or a reflective set of realistic options. It regaled them with pep rallies, demonstrations, and literature.

"But it was blue smoke and mirrors, balloons and hot air. It lacked the substance and clout to force the company's hand in bargaining, but it stung sufficiently to cause anger, bitterness, and an unwise rigidity and hawkishness in corporate headquarters.

"In the short run Rogers and Guyette successfully manipulated a democratic institution, respectful of local autonomy, by *securing majority support* [of the P-9 rank and file]. The propaganda stream has been imaginative and unceasing. In their use of the technique of repetition establishing truth, they would have made Joseph Paul Goebbels' Nazi propaganda ministry envious." (Emphasis added.)

The International officers here as elsewhere in their attacks focused on Rogers and Guyette, but what really bothered them was the undeniable fact that they couldn't crack the majority of the rank and file. Their next move was simply to overrule that majority.

Above: Workers and supporters from Ottumwa, Iowa, at Austin
march, April 12, 1986. Below: Austin youth supporting P-9.

According to Wynn, on March 4, 1986, the UFCW International Executive Committee unilaterally lifted sanction of the strike by P-9 against the Hormel company, effective March 14. The board issued a directive to the Local P-9 officers to "cease the strike and all related strike activities, including the unsanctioned extension of picket lines to other facilities and the unsanctioned boycott of Hormel products, and to make an offer to return to work on behalf of all remaining strikers. . . ."

The directive also declared that benefits would cease for those continuing to strike but that "the International union and Region 13 will pay post-strike assistance to replaced strikers who do not violate this directive by unauthorized picketing or carrying on the unauthorized boycott."

The membership of Local P-9 met March 16 and voted to continue the strike and strike-related activities including the boycott.

On March 19, 1986, UFCW President William Wynn sent a letter to the members of P-9 instructing them to make an unconditional offer to the company to return to work immediately. The International officers also sent two form letters that members were instructed to fill out and send in. One was to the company making an unconditional offer to return to work and the other to the International Union requesting "post-strike benefits." The latter had a box at the bottom to check if the member had sent in the unconditional offer to return to work. The International Union officers were now paying benefits to P-9 members only if they offered to scab.

* * *

On March 24 Wynn informed P-9 that proceedings were beginning to place the Local under trusteeship. The grounds were that the Local had defied the March 13 directive to halt all strike activity and offer to return to work on company terms. The terms were the contract the company implemented after the strike began and under which the scabs were working. The contract gutted the in-plant seniority system, eliminated the guaranteed annual wage and the fifty-two-week layoff notice, provided for hiring temporary part-time workers without benefits, left safety matters entirely up to the judgment of the company, and contained a two-tier wage system with a permanent dollar less an hour for all new hires. Thus, the basic wage was $10 an hour for workers who were there before the strike. New hires began at $8; received $8.50 after six months; and $9 from then on, with no cost-of-living allowance.

The terms included keeping the scabs, with no guarantee of rehiring for any strikers.

Thus the UFCW International officers took the unprecedented step of using the trusteeship procedure to break a strike.

In mid-April the International Union conducted a hearing in Minneapolis on the trusteeship. The hearing officer refused to take testimony on the substance of the matter, confining the evidence to whether or not the Local had defied the March 13 directive. The outcome was therefore cut and dried. On May 9, 1986, the UFCW International Executive Committee imposed trusteeship on Local P-9, suspending its officers and replacing them with an appointed trustee, Joseph T. Hansen. According to the trusteeship terms, Hansen need not call membership meetings and had full powers to rule the Local as a dictator for eighteen months. The International officers did not have enough support in Austin to enforce this, however. They appealed in federal court for an order enforcing the terms. Local P-9 sought an injunction against the trusteeship from the same court.

In the meantime P-9 carried on the strike, including picketing, boycott, and support activities.

On April 11, P-9 members and supporters were attacked by police in front of the plant and eventually dispersed with tear gas. There were eighteen arrests, including Guyette and Rogers. All eighteen face "felony riot" charges. (Earlier, on February 6, twenty-seven pickets had been arrested near the plant gate and Ray Rogers was charged with "criminal syndicalism,"a state law felony carrying a five-year jail term. The National Emergency Civil Liberties Committee took up Rogers's case, arguing that the law violated the U.S. Constitution. In April, the charge was dropped.)

On April 12, a march of more than 5,000 P-9 members and supporters, including unionists from forty states, took place in the streets of Austin. A rally later that day was addressed by officials from union locals around the country, as well as a leader of a Missouri farmers' organization. The following afternoon, Jesse Jackson spoke before a follow-up rally of 1,000 at a local church.

Due to pressure from trustee Hansen, some P-9 strikers who were behind on their mortgage payments received notices from banks that unless they signed the unconditional return-to-work letter, they faced foreclosure on their homes.

Through all this the P-9 strikers, now about 900, remained solid, subsisting on the funds, food, and clothing they raised through their own efforts and that of their supporters. The Local's communications committee continued sending speakers around the country.

On June 2, U.S. District Judge Edward Devitt ruled the trusteeship valid and issued a court order requiring the Local's officers to relinquish their posts, refrain from any strike activity, and turn over to the trustee the Local's property, including offices, records, and finances.

Facing federal felony convictions if they violated the court order, the P-9 officers complied under strong protest.[9]

Official P-9 pickets were removed from the plant and the records and keys to the offices turned over to the trustee.

Hansen made a blanket offer to the company declaring that all P-9 members were ready to return to work unconditionally. The company, however, did not call them back. The state authorities then ruled the unemployed Hormel workers were eligible for unemployment compensation.

Trustee Hansen and his deputies did not at the time occupy the union offices in the Austin Labor Center. Instead they operated from a small storefront a few blocks away on Main Street.

They had the bank freeze all P-9 funds, got the post office to impound P-9's mail and any addressed to the suspended officers that came to the labor center, had the phone company shut off all telephone service that was under P-9's name, and got garbage collection stopped. Hansen also

---

9. At the time they were forced to relinquish their posts, the officers of Local P-9 were: President James Guyette, Vice President Lynn Huston, Financial Secretary Kathy Buck, Business Agent Peter Winkels, and Executive Board members Floyd Lenoch, James Retterath, Carl Pontius, and John "Skinny" Weis.

Though this was the "new" leadership elected between 1980 and 1985, it was not without extensive experience in the industry. All but Huston and Buck had worked in the old plant as well as the new. Huston was hired in 1982, Buck in 1983. Before that Buck worked nine years in the company headquarters.

Guyette had seventeen years, Winkels and Retterath eighteen, Lenoch thirty-nine, and Weis forty-two, working at the Austin plants. Carl Pontius had twenty years at the Hormel plant in Ft. Dodge, Iowa, which closed in 1981. He also worked at the Dallas plant before transferring to Austin. At Ft. Dodge he had held office while the local there was in the United Packinghouse Workers, and later in the Amalgamated Meat Cutters.

tried to seize the funds of the United Support Group.

Just at this time the P-9 membership and the support group were organizing a week-long encampment in Austin, called Solidarity City, for June 23 through 28. They operated out of the remainder of the Austin Labor Center where the strike kitchen, meeting hall, and offices of the United Support Group were still located. (The trustee and his deputies held the keys only to the P-9 offices proper.)

The harassment by the trustee backed by the federal court order put a real crimp in this organizing effort, particularly the lack of adequate telephones for a period of about two weeks. Nevertheless, Solidarity City was a modest success, capped off with a march of more than a thousand, including supporting unionists from some thirty states.

Among other things Solidarity City was an important educational experience. Discussions took place among unionists and activists from other movements and with featured speakers like Monsignor Charles Owens Rice, the prolabor priest from Pittsburgh; Vernon Bellecourt of the American Indian Movement; Crystal Lee Sutton, the real "Norma Rae"; Carla Whittington of the National Organization for Women; Jerry Parks, of the Chillicothe, Missouri farmers' struggle; and anti-apartheid activist Enoch Duma.[10]

Several times during Solidarity City, P-9ers pointed to

---

10. "During the year, new technical service and licensing agreements were established with Renown Food Products Corp. of the Republic of South Africa, and with HaiTai Confectionery Company Ltd. of the Republic of South Africa."—From the Geo. A. Hormel & Co. Annual Report, 1984.

South African workers at Renown are organized by the Sweet, Food and Allied Workers Union (SFAWU), affiliated to the Congress of South African Trade Unions (COSATU). SFAWU General Secretary David Makhema said his union wished to "express solidarity with the Hormel strikers—we will do everything we can to help them." He also said Renown is "totally anti-union."

the important role of the women who have built support for the struggle against Hormel through the United Support Group.

Jan Butts, president of the group, has explained the impact of involvement in the strike on these women: "Women are now coming to meetings and speaking out who never thought they had the capability. They are standing up for what they really believe."

Also present during the week's activities were members of P-9 Future Generation, a local support group formed by Austin high school students.

* * *

During the discussions at Solidarity City, P-9ers explained their latest move in the fight against Hormel. The UFCW International officials had carried out a sustained, public campaign over a couple of years to crush the rebellion by Local P-9. The imposition of Hansen's dictatorship over the Local and calling off the strike were the most recent attacks in that campaign. Once again, the membership of P-9 was faced with two choices: give up or deepen the struggle. Once again they chose the latter course.

Hundreds of them filed a petition with the National Labor Relations Board (NLRB) to recertify themselves as a new union. They called it "Original P-9."

This new union would give the P-9 membership a democratic form through which to continue the struggle for a decent contract from Hormel and for a militant, rank-and-file controlled union in the meat-packing industry.

P-9 members explained to their supporters that they did not take lightly the decision to organize outside the UFCW. But the officialdom's moves to place them outside the union and to mobilize vast resources to try to drum them out of the labor movement gave the Austin meat-packers no alternative.

Shortly after Solidarity City ended, the federal court in St. Paul ruled that the Austin Labor Center was part of the assets under control of the UFCW trustee. On July 2, 1986, P-9ers were told that the trustee would occupy the union hall that afternoon. Within hours the United Support Group moved to another building two blocks down the street and carried on their support activities.

Around the same time the National Labor Relations Board in Minneapolis informed the filers of the "Original P-9" petition that it would be rejected within a week on the grounds that the name was too close to that of the trusteed UFCW Local P-9.

The name was changed to North American Meat Packers Union (NAMPU), a new petition drawn up, signatures obtained, and filed before the deadline. An office of NAMPU was also opened nearby. Supporters of NAMPU saw in it the potential to link up, through common struggle, with other workers in the Hormel chain, as well as with meat-packers who work for other companies.

* * *

Since they had not yet had time to fix up a hall suitable for large meetings, the members and their supporters met the evening of July 2 at Sutton Park. Three of the speakers were John Winkels, his brother Casper, and Casper's son, Pete. John Winkels recalled that this was the same park the workers had met in that July evening fifty-three years ago when they organized Local 1 of the Independent Union of All Workers.

Connie Dammen, who worked in the new plant before the strike, told the meeting: "They've taken away our name.

Retired members of Local P-9 organize in support of the strike.

"P-9 Future Generation" name of organization of Austin high school students supporting the strike.

They've taken away the union hall we've all come to love. But the hall is bricks and mortar. They can't take the people and the union is the people."

The meeting resolved to carry on the struggle.

July 7, 1986
Austin, Minnesota

Afterword

In some ways the members of Local P-9 are unique. Until the voracious concessionary drive of the Hormel company from 1978 through 1985, they had considerably higher incomes than most U.S. workers. They worked harder at a more difficult, dirty, and dangerous job. They had a stronger local union and more dignity at work. Many of them were second and third generation Hormel workers.

A far higher proportion of them owned their own homes. Because of the early militancy of their local union, they lived in a town in which a higher percentage of all the workers enjoyed union benefits than is the case in most small towns in the United States—or big cities, for that matter. In large part because of this, they were the products of a good educational system, of decent social services, and their town had no slums. They were literate and articulate. And their expectations were high.

Because of all this, when the blows of the employers' offensive hit them, they felt it deeply and eventually reacted by organizing a more serious fight than has yet been the case elsewhere in this period.

Most important, they were able to throw up a fighting leadership from within their own ranks and to obtain some expert help and training from advisers of their own choosing. This meant they were not dependent for aid and advice upon International Union officers who were alien to the membership and alien to the very idea of putting up a serious struggle against the corporations. They were able to reach out and sustain themselves morally and materially on solidarity instead of being left alone to twist in the wind, as so many other brave rank-and-file fighters have been.

Those P-9 strikers who have stuck it out have become transformed. They have a slogan: "Some people went on strike for themself, and went back. Some people went on strike for others, and stayed out."

Many of their number have traveled to distant places to speak to hundreds of other local unions, and to various organizations of farmers, women, Blacks, and students to build solidarity for the fight. And they touched a responsive chord across the country and overseas. They broke through some of the barriers that divide working people. They no longer consider themselves just as citizens of Austin, but as citizens of the world. They know Hormel has interests in South Africa, and they dedicated the new mural on the outside wall of their union hall to Nelson Mandela, the most prominent leader of the anti-apartheid struggle, who has been in a South African prison for twenty-two years.

But they are actually not so exceptional. Theirs is really a classic case. What the company did to them is also happening to the rest of the working class, and it's going to continue and get worse until the labor movement stops it.

As this is being written, the original P-9ers and their supporters are carrying on the struggle through two forms: the United Support Group and the North American Meat Packers Union. The petitions filed by NAMPU supporters have been accepted by the National Labor Relations Board, which is now legally obligated to set a date within a reasonable period of time for a recertification election at the Austin Hormel plant.

The trusteed UFCW Local P-9 will be on the ballot. NAMPU will also be on the ballot. In addition, workers will be able to vote to have no union.

A competition to win allegiance and votes in the forth-coming election is now under way. Both sides have been holding meetings to present their respective positions and to appeal for support among those working in the plant as well as among strikers who have not been hired back, but are still legally part of the work force for purposes of the election.

NAMPU organizers are also contacting workers in other meat-packing plants, including those in the Hormel chain, to discuss a serious fight for decent contracts, as well as for a democratic, industrial union of meat-packers. All this takes place in the context of a number of contracts expiring this fall in the meat-packing industry. This puts pressure on the officials of the UFCW International and on the cor-porations. The struggle continues to unfold.

* * *

These Austin meat-packers are struggling, now, to trans-form the U.S. labor movement into what it ought to be, a fighting instrument in the hands of the rank and file. This is a fight of historic proportions—one whose inevitability has been mounting for forty years. It is a fight that every working person has a stake in.

The Austin packinghouse workers are proof of what U.S. labor can be and what it must become. Their determination and far-sightedness merit the emulation of every worker. They and their fellow meat-packers in Ottumwa and Fre-mont deserve everyone's support.

July 25, 1986
Los Angeles

SELECTED CHRONOLOGY OF EVENTS

1933

July – Union recognized at Hormel plant in Austin, MN

November – First sit-down strike of 1930s takes place at Hormel

1940

Hormel and United Packinghouse Workers of America Local No. 9, CIO, sign Permanent Working Agreement, which lasts for thirty-eight years

1978

United Food and Commercial Workers Local P-9 negotiates concessions agreement with Hormel to build new plant in Austin

1981

UFCW officials negotiate wage-freeze contract for Hormel locals

1982

August 9 – New Austin plant opens

1984

May – Top UFCW official approves separate negotiations with Hormel by UFCW Local 431 in Ottumwa, Iowa; this breaks solidarity of locals in Hormel chain, putting contract expiration dates out of sync

September – Meetings of Hormel locals (Local P-9 is excluded) agree to concessions on Ottumwa pattern

October 8–Hormel imposes 23 percent wage cuts on Local P-9

1985

January 18–P-9 members vote to assess themselves $3 each per week to hire Ray Rogers's Corporate Campaign, Inc.

February–P-9 members begin traveling to other meat-packing plants in Midwest to discuss issues

August 14–P-9 votes to reject Hormel's final contract offer

August 16–UFCW position paper publicly attacks P-9

August 17–1,500 Austin meat-packers strike Hormel

August 20–Hormel announces 83 percent rise in profits

October 19–P-9 votes unanimously to support any union member honoring roving picket lines

November–Officers of most locals in Hormel chain ask UFCW International to sanction extension of picket lines; UFCW President William Wynn publicly refuses

December–UFCW International officials insist on acceptance of mediator's contract agreed to by Hormel; P-9 votes it down twice

1986

January 13–Hormel opens plant gates to scabs; Wynn publicly demands P-9 go back to work

January 21–UFCW International officials release "fact book" defending Hormel and slandering Local P-9

January 23–National Guard escorts scabs through picket line

January 26–P-9 calls for boycott of Hormel products

January 27–P-9 sends roving pickets to other Hormel plants, including Ottumwa and Fremont, Nebraska

February 6–Twenty-seven pickets arrested near Austin plant gate; Ray Rogers charged with "criminal syndicalism"

February 15–Pro–P-9 rally of 3,000 in Austin

February 21–P-9 removes pickets from Ottumwa; those fired try to return to work, but company locks them out

March 14–UFCW International Executive Committee lifting of strike sanction goes into effect; officials order P-9 to cease strike and boycott; strike benefits to Local cut off

March 16–P-9 votes to continue strike

April 11–Police riot at plant gate; eighteen strikers and supporters arrested

April 12–More than 5,000 P-9 members and supporters march through Austin

May 9–UFCW officials impose trusteeship on P-9; Joseph T. Hansen takes over Local

June 2–Federal Judge Edward Devitt upholds trusteeship

June 5–Over 30 percent of P-9 members sign petitions with NLRB asking for a union recertification election to make "Original P-9" bargaining agent for Austin Hormel workers

June 23–28–United Support Group organizes Solidarity City, which culminates in march of 1,000 in Austin

July 3–UFCW trustee occupies Austin Labor Center

July 7–North American Meat Packers Union organizers announce they've filed union recertification petitions after NLRB indicates it would reject "Original P-9" petitions (NLRB subsequently accepts new petition)

Is Socialist Revolution in the U.S. Possible?
A Necessary Debate
MARY-ALICE WATERS

In two talks, presented as part of a wide-ranging debate at the Venezuela International Book Fairs in 2007 and 2008, Waters explains why a socialist revolution in the United States is possible. Why revolutionary struggles by working people are inevitable, forced upon us by the crisis-driven assaults of the propertied classes. As solidarity grows among a fighting vanguard of working people, the outlines of coming class battles can already be seen. $7. Also in Spanish, French, and Swedish.

Cuba and the Coming American Revolution
JACK BARNES

The Cuban Revolution of 1959 had a worldwide political impact, including on working people and youth in the imperialist heartland. As the mass, proletarian-based struggle for Black rights was already advancing in the US, the social transformation fought for and won by the Cuban toilers set an example that socialist revolution is not only necessary—it can be made and defended.

This second edition, with a new foreword by Mary-Alice Waters, should be read alongside *Is Socialist Revolution in the U.S. Possible?* $10. Also in Spanish and French.

www.pathfinderpress.com

Building a PROLETARIAN PARTY

The History of American Trotskyism, 1928–1938
Report of a Participant
JAMES P. CANNON

"Trotskyism is not a new movement, a new doctrine," Cannon says, "but the restoration, the revival of genuine Marxism as it was expounded and practiced in the Russian revolution and in the early days of the Communist International." In twelve talks given in 1942, Cannon recounts a decisive period in efforts to build a proletarian party in the United States. $22. Also in Spanish and French.

Revolutionary Continuity
Marxist Leadership in the U.S.
FARRELL DOBBS

How successive generations took part in struggles of the US labor movement, seeking to build a leadership that could advance the class interests of workers and small farmers and link up with fellow toilers around the world. Two volumes:

The Early Years, 1848–1917, $20; _Birth of the Communist Movement 1918–1922_, $19.

The Struggle for a Proletarian Party
JAMES P. CANNON

"The workers of America have power enough to topple the structure of capitalism at home and to lift the whole world with them when they rise," Cannon asserts. On the eve of World War II, a founder of the communist movement in the US and leader of the Communist International in Lenin's time defends the program and party-building norms of Bolshevism. $22

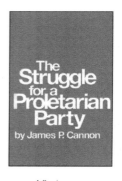

THE TEAMSTER SERIES

FARRELL DOBBS, *a young worker who became part of the class-struggle leadership of the Minneapolis Teamsters in the 1930s tells the story of how the strikes and organizing drives by men and women in the Twin Cities and throughout the Midwest paved the way for the rise of the industrial union movement. They showed in life what workers and their allied producers on the land can achieve when they have the leadership they deserve.*

Teamster Rebellion

How members of Teamsters Local 574 in Minnesota during two 1934 strikes defeated not only the trucking bosses in Minneapolis but strike-breaking efforts of the big-business Citizens Alliance and city, state, and federal governments. $19. Also in Spanish, French, and Swedish.

Teamster Power

How the class-struggle Teamsters leadership used the power workers had won during the 1934 strikes to make Minneapolis a union town and launch an 11-state campaign that brought tens of thousands of over-the-road truckers into the union. $19. Also in Spanish.

Teamster Politics

How the Minneapolis Teamsters combated FBI frame-ups, helped the jobless organize, deployed a Union Defense Guard to turn back fascist thugs, fought to advance independent labor political action, and mobilized opposition to US imperialism's entry into World War II. $19

Teamster Bureaucracy

How the employing class, backed by union bureaucrats, stepped up government efforts to gag class-conscious militants; how workers mounted a world campaign to free eighteen union and socialist leaders framed up and imprisoned in the infamous 1941 federal sedition trial. $19

www.pathfinderpress.com

From the dictatorship of capital...

The Communist Manifesto

Karl Marx, Frederick Engels

Founding document of the modern revolutionary workers movement, published in 1848. Why communism is not a set of preconceived principles but the line of march of the working class toward power—a line of march "springing from an existing class struggle, a historical movement going on under our very eyes." $5. Also in Spanish, French, and Arabic.

State and Revolution

V.I. Lenin

"The relation of the socialist proletarian revolution to the state is acquiring not only practical political importance," wrote V.I. Lenin in this booklet just months before the October 1917 Russian Revolution. It also addresses the "most urgent problem of the day: explaining to the masses what they will have to do to free themselves from capitalist tyranny." In *Essential Works of Lenin.* $12.95

Their Trotsky and Ours

Jack Barnes

To lead the working class in a successful revolution, a mass proletarian party is needed whose cadres, well beforehand, have absorbed a world communist program, are proletarian in life and work, derive deep satisfaction from doing politics, and have forged a leadership with an acute sense of what to do next. This book is about building such a party. $16. Also in Spanish and French.

www.pathfinderpress.com

...to the dictatorship of the proletariat

Lenin's Final Fight

Speeches and Writings, 1922–23

V.I. Lenin

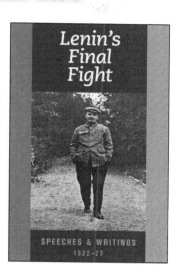

In 1922 and 1923, V.I. Lenin, central leader of the world's first socialist revolution, waged what was to be his last political battle. At stake was whether that revolution would remain on the proletarian course that had brought workers and peasants to power in October 1917—and laid the foundations for a truly worldwide revolutionary movement of toilers organizing to emulate the Bolsheviks' example. $20. Also in Spanish.

Trade Unions: Their Past, Present, and Future

Karl Marx

Apart from being instruments "required for guerrilla fights between capital and labor," the unions "must now act deliberately as organizing centers of the working class in the broad interest of its complete emancipation," through revolutionary political action. Drafted by Marx for the First International's founding congress in 1866, this resolution appears in *Trade Unions in the Epoch of Imperialist Decay* by Leon Trotsky. $16

The History of the Russian Revolution

Leon Trotsky

The social, economic, and political dynamics of the first socialist revolution as told by one of its central leaders. How, under Lenin's leadership, the Bolshevik Party led the overturn of the monarchist regime of the landlords and capitalists and brought to power a government of the workers and peasants. Unabridged, 3 vols. in one. $38. Also in Russian.

"What Cuba can give the world is its example"
—THE SECOND DECLARATION OF HAVANA

Soldier of the Cuban Revolution

From the Cane Fields of Oriente to General of the Revolutionary Armed Forces
LUIS ALFONSO ZAYAS

The author recounts his experiences over five decades in the revolution. From a teenage combatant in the clandestine struggle and 1956–58 war that brought down the US-backed dictatorship, to serving three times as a leader of the Cuban volunteer forces that helped Angola defeat an invasion by the army of white-supremacist South Africa, Zayas tells how ordinary men and women in Cuba changed the course of history and, in the process, transformed themselves as well. $18. Also in Spanish.

Our History Is Still Being Written

The Story of Three Chinese–Cuban Generals in the Cuban Revolution

Armando Choy, Gustavo Chui, and Moisés Sío Wong talk about the historic place of Chinese immigration to Cuba, as well as over five decades of revolutionary action and internationalism, from Cuba to Angola and Venezuela today. Through their stories we see the social and political forces that gave birth to the Cuban nation and opened the door to socialist revolution in the Americas. $20. Also in Spanish and Chinese.

The First and Second Declarations of Havana

Nowhere are the questions of revolutionary strategy that today confront men and women on the front lines of struggles in the Americas addressed with greater truthfulness and clarity than in these uncompromising indictments of imperialist plunder and "the exploitation of man by man." Adopted by million-strong assemblies of the Cuban people in 1960 and 1962. $10. Also in Spanish, French, and Arabic.

www.pathfinderpress.com

Che Guevara Talks to Young People

ERNESTO CHE GUEVARA

In eight talks from 1959 to 1964, the Argentine-born revolutionary challenges youth of Cuba and the world to study, to work, to become disciplined. To join the front lines of struggles, small and large. To politicize their organizations and themselves. To become a different kind of human being as they strive together with working people of all lands to transform the world. $15. Also in Spanish.

Playa Girón/Bay of Pigs

Washington's First Military Defeat in the Americas

FIDEL CASTRO, JOSÉ RAMÓN FERNÁNDEZ

In fewer than 72 hours of combat in April 1961, Cuba's revolutionary armed forces defeated a US-organized invasion by 1,500 mercenaries. In the process, the Cuban people set an example for workers, farmers, and youth the world over that with political consciousness, class solidarity, courage, and revolutionary leadership, one can stand up to enormous might and seemingly insurmountable odds—*and win*. $22. Also in Spanish.

Marianas in Combat

Teté Puebla and the Mariana Grajales Women's Platoon in Cuba's Revolutionary War 1956–58

TETÉ PUEBLA

Brigadier General Teté Puebla, the highest-ranking woman in Cuba's Revolutionary Armed Forces, joined the struggle to overthrow the US-backed dictatorship of Fulgencio Batista in 1956, when she was fifteen years old. This is her story—from clandestine action in the cities, to serving as an officer in the victorious Rebel Army's first all-women's unit—the Mariana Grajales Women's Platoon. For nearly fifty years, the fight to transform the social and economic status of women in Cuba has been inseparable from Cuba's socialist revolution. $14. Also in Spanish.

Dynamics of the Cuban Revolution

A Marxist Appreciation

JOSEPH HANSEN

How did the Cuban Revolution unfold? Why does it represent an "unbearable challenge" to US imperialism? What political obstacles has it overcome? Written as the revolution advanced from its earliest days. $25

New International
A MAGAZINE OF MARXIST POLITICS AND THEORY

NEW INTERNATIONAL NO. 12

Capitalism's Long Hot Winter Has Begun

Jack Barnes

and "Their Transformation and Ours,"
Resolution of the Socialist Workers Party
Today's sharpening interimperialist conflicts are fueled both by the opening stages of what will be decades of economic, financial, and social convulsions and class battles, and by the most far-reaching shift in Washington's military policy and organization since the US buildup toward World War II. Class-struggle-minded working people must face this historic turning point for imperialism, and draw satisfaction from being "in their face" as we chart a revolutionary course to confront it. $16

NEW INTERNATIONAL NO. 14

The Clintons' Antilabor Legacy: Roots of the 2008 World Financial Crisis

Jack Barnes

Examines the consequences for the working class of the Democratic Party's antilabor shift on domestic policy in the closing years of the twentieth century, and the Democratic-Republican convergence on this and other issues during the presidency of William Clinton.

Also in No. 14: "Revolution, Internationalism, and Socialism: The Last Year of Malcolm X"; "The Stewardship of Nature Also Falls to the Working Class"; and "Setting the Record Straight on Fascism and World War II." $14

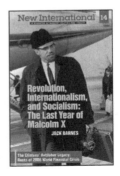

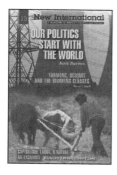

NEW INTERNATIONAL NO. 13

OUR POLITICS START WITH THE WORLD

Jack Barnes

The huge economic and cultural inequalities between imperialist and semicolonial countries, and among classes within almost every country, are produced, reproduced, and accentuated by the workings of capitalism. For vanguard workers to build parties able to lead a successful revolutionary struggle for power in our own countries, says Jack Barnes in the lead article, our activity must be guided by a strategy to close this gap.

Also in No. 13: "Farming, Science, and the Working Classes" *by Steve Clark.* $14

NEW INTERNATIONAL NO. 11

U.S. IMPERIALISM HAS LOST THE COLD WAR

Jack Barnes

Contrary to imperialist expectations at the opening of the 1990s in the wake of the collapse of regimes across Eastern Europe and the USSR claiming to be communist, the workers and farmers there have not been crushed. The toilers remain an intractable obstacle to imperialism's advance, one the exploiters will have to confront in class battles and war. $16

NEW INTERNATIONAL NO. 8

CHE GUEVARA, CUBA, AND THE ROAD TO SOCIALISM

Articles by Ernesto Che Guevara, Carlos Rafael Rodríguez, Carlos Tablada, Mary-Alice Waters, Steve Clark, Jack Barnes

Exchanges from the opening years of the Cuban Revolution and today on the political perspectives defended by Guevara as he helped lead working people to advance the transformation of economic and social relations in Cuba. $10

NEW INTERNATIONAL NO. 5

THE COMING REVOLUTION IN SOUTH AFRICA

Jack Barnes

Writing a decade before the white supremacist regime fell, Barnes explores the social roots of apartheid in South African capitalism and tasks of urban and rural toilers in dismantling it, as they forge a communist leadership of the working class. $14

EXPAND *your Revolutionary Library*

The Working Class and the Transformation of Learning
The Fraud of Education Reform under Capitalism
JACK BARNES

"Until society is reorganized so that education is a human activity from the time we are very young until the time we die, there will be no education worthy of working, creating humanity." $3. Also in Spanish, French, Swedish, Icelandic, Farsi, and Greek.

Malcolm X Talks to Young People

"You're living at a time of revolution," Malcolm told young people in the United Kingdom in December 1964. "And I for one will join in with anyone, I don't care what color you are, as long as you want to change the miserable condition that exists on this earth." Four talks and an interview given to young people in Ghana, the UK, and the United States in the last months of Malcolm's life. $15. Also in Spanish and French.

Problems of Women's Liberation
EVELYN REED

Six articles explore the social and economic roots of women's oppression from prehistoric society to modern capitalism and point the road forward to emancipation. $15